Going Through

The Storms

of

Life

Isaiah 43:1-2

By

JULIUS R. MALONE

© 2007 by
Julius R Malone

All Scripture quotations are taken from the New King James
Version of The Holy Bible unless otherwise indicated.

ISBN 978-1-60530-692-6

Printed in the United States of America

CONTENTS

Dedication

This book is dedicated to my darling wife Ann who has stood by me through every storm during our marriage of over fifty years.

Acknowledgements

Thanks to all of those who read this manuscript and offered helpful suggestions: my wife Ann, my daughter Debbie Lassiter, John Fisco, Rita Bertolas, Barbara Farrow, Beverly Taylor, Kathy Gaillard, and Sandra Mack. I also thank the members of the New Testament Church for their prayers and encouragement to publish some of my sermons.

Introduction

On the voyage of life, everyone will encounter some storms - both literal and figurative. The figurative storms are the difficulties, disappointments, discouragements, depressions, and disasters that are common to all who sail the sea of life.

The Bible teaches that believers are not exempt from the storms of tribulations, trials, troubles, temptations, and tragedies of life. Jesus said, "These things I have spoken to you, that in Me you may have peace. In the world you will have tribulation; but be of good cheer, I have overcome the world" (John 16:33, NKJ). David said: "Many are the afflictions of the righteous, but the Lord delivers him out of them all" (Ps. 34:19, NKJ). Paul reminds us that temptations and trials are common: "No temptation has overtaken you except such as is common to man; but God is faithful, who will not allow you to be tempted beyond what you are able, but with the temptation will also make the way of escape, that you may be able to bear it" (1 Cor. 10:13, NKJ). Paul also points out that God sometimes appoints afflictions and that believers should expect tribulation and persecution: "That no one should be shaken by these afflictions; for you yourselves know that we are appointed to this. For, in fact, we told you before when we were with you that we would suffer tribulation, just as it happened, and you know" (1 Thess. 3:3-4, NKJ). "Yes, and all who desire to live godly in Christ Jesus will suffer persecution" (2 Tim. 3:12, NKJ). James tells Christians what to do, not if, but when the storms of the trials of life come: "My brethren, count it all joy when you fall into various trials, knowing that the testing of your faith produces patience. But let patience have its perfect work, that you may be perfect and complete, lacking nothing" (James 1:2-4, NKJ). Peter also warns Christians to expect the storms of trials and suffering: "Beloved, do not think it strange concerning the fiery trial which is to try you, as though some strange thing happened to you" (1 Pet. 4:12, NKJ). "But may the God of all grace, who called us to His eternal glory by Christ Jesus, after you have suffered a while, perfect, establish, strengthen, and settle you" (1 Pet. 5:10, NKJ).

I believe that God has one or more purposes for every literal or figurative storm that He produces or permits in one's life. Although we cannot always satisfactorily answer the question "why?" this book will examine some of God's purposes for storms in our lives. As you shall see, God may use storms to disclose, develop, discipline, direct, and draw.

Chapter 1

The Necessity of Going Though Some Storms

In June, 1988, I experienced a mild heart attack, and I was admitted to the hospital for the first time as a patient. I prayed for God to give me a word from the Bible that would help me to go through the hospital experience. The Holy Spirit immediately brought to my mind Isaiah 43:1-3, NKJ:

But now, thus says the LORD, who created you, O Jacob, and He who formed you, O Israel: "Fear not, for I have redeemed you; I have called you by your name; you are mine. When you pass through the waters, I will be with you; and through the rivers, they shall not overflow you. When you walk through the fire, you shall not be burned, nor shall the flame scorch you. For I am the LORD your God, the Holy One of Israel, your Savior; I gave Egypt for your ransom, Ethiopia and Seba in your place."

The words that stood out in this passage were "when," "through," and "I will be with you." I found comfort in the reminders of these facts: First, God is my Creator and Redeemer. I belong to God. It is important to be able to say, "I have been redeemed." The psalmist said, "Let the redeemed of the LORD say so" (Ps. 107:2a, NKJ). When one is going through a storm, death is the worst that can happen; but if one has been redeemed, then death means to be absent from the body is to be present with the Lord (2 Cor. 5:8, NKJ).

Second, God knows my name. In fact, there is not anything about me that God does not know. David said, "O Lord, You have searched me and known me. You know my sitting down and my rising up; You understand my thought afar off. You comprehend my path and my lying down, and are acquainted with all my ways" (Ps. 139:1-3, NKJ). God knows who I am, where I am, and what I am going through.

Third, there is the promise of the presence of God, not if, but when I go through the storms of life. No storm is too difficult when God is with me. God keeps His promises, and peace is found in the promise of His presence. David said, "Yea, though I walk through the valley of the shadow of death, I will fear no evil; for You are with me; Your rod and Your staff, they comfort me" (Ps. 23:4, NKJ).

When I am in a storm, I still find comfort and strength in Isaiah 43:1-3. Since 1988, I have read this passage to hospital patients more than any other passage in the Bible, and I believe that this passage has brought comfort and strength to many.

The Bible teaches that there are some storms through

which God wants us to go for His glory and for our good. For example, God took Joseph through the pit and the prison before promoting him to the palace in Egypt (Gen. 37:23-29; 39:20; 41:38-44). Through all of the storms, God was with Joseph (Gen. 39:2-3, 21-23). Joseph later said to his brothers, "But as for you, you meant evil against me; but God meant it for good, in order to bring it about as it is this day, to save many people alive" (Gen. 50:20, NKJ).

God took the Hebrews through the Red Sea on dry ground:

Then Moses stretched out his hand over the sea; and the LORD caused the sea to go back by a strong east wind all that night, and made the sea into dry land, and the waters were divided. So the children of Israel went into the midst of the sea on the dry ground, and the waters were a wall to them on their right hand and on their left (Ex. 14:21-22, NKJ).

Observe how God was glorified after the Hebrews crossed the Red Sea:

Then Moses and the children of Israel sang this song to the LORD, and spoke, saying: "I will sing to the LORD for He has triumphed gloriously! The horse and its rider He has thrown into the sea! The LORD is my strength and song, and He has become my salvation; He is my God, and I will praise Him; my father's God, and I will exalt Him. The LORD is a man of war; the LORD is His name. Pharaoh's chariots and his army He has cast into the sea; His

3

chosen captains also are drowned in the Red Sea. The depths have covered them; they sank to the bottom like a stone. Your right hand, O LORD, has become glorious in power; Your right hand, O LORD, has dashed the enemy in pieces. And in the greatness of Your excellence You have overthrown those who rose against You; You sent forth Your wrath; it consumed them like stubble. And with the blast of Your nostrils the waters were gathered together; the floods stood upright like a heap; the depths congealed in the heart of the sea. The enemy said, 'I will pursue, I will overtake, I will divide the spoil; my desire shall be satisfied on them. I will draw my sword, my hand shall destroy them.' You blew with Your wind, the sea covered them; they sank like lead in the mighty waters. Who is like You, O LORD, among the gods? Who is like You, glorious in holiness, fearful in praises, doing wonders? You stretched out Your right hand; the earth swallowed them. You in Your mercy have led forth the people whom You have redeemed; You have guided them in Your strength to Your holy habitation. The people will hear and be afraid; sorrow will take hold of the inhabitants of Philistia. Then the chiefs of Edom will be dismayed; the mighty men of Moab, trembling will take hold of them; all the inhabitants of Canaan will melt away. Fear and dread will fall on them; by the greatness of Your arm they will be as still as a stone, till Your people pass over, O LORD, till the people pass over whom You have purchased.You will bring them in and plant them in the mountain of Your inheritance, in the place, O LORD, which You have made for Your own dwelling, the sanctuary, O LORD, which Your hands have established. The LORD shall reign forever and ever. For the horses of Pharaoh went with his chariots and his horsemen into the sea, and the LORD brought back the waters of the sea upon them. But the children of Israel went on dry land in the midst of the sea." Then Miriam the prophetess, the sister

of Aaron, took the timbrel in her hand; and all the women went out after her with timbrels and with dances. And Miriam answered them: "Sing to the Lord, for He has triumphed gloriously! The horse and its rider He has thrown into the sea!" (Exodus 15:1-21, NKJ).

God took David through the valley of the shadow of death. God was with David when David fought a lion, a bear, and the giant Goliath (1 Sam. 17:32-51). David found comfort in God's manifest presence as he went through the storms in his life. Many of the Psalms of David that are still blessing many today were written when David was fleeing for his life from King Saul and later from his son Absalom. For example, Psalms 3 and 61 are two of the Psalms written in relation to the rebellion of David's son Absalom:

LORD, how they have increased who trouble me! Many are they who rise up against me. Many are they who say of me, "There is no help for him in God." Selah. But You, O LORD, are a shield for me, my glory and the One who lifts up my head. I cried to the LORD with my voice, and He heard me from His holy hill. Selah. I lay down and slept; I awoke, for the LORD sustained me. I will not be afraid of ten thousands of people who have set themselves against me all around. Arise, O LORD; save me, O my God! For You have struck all my enemies on the cheekbone; You have broken the teeth of the ungodly. Salvation belongs to the LORD. Your blessing is upon Your people. Selah (Ps. 3:1-8, NKJ).

Hear my cry, O God; attend to my prayer. From the end of the earth I will cry to You, when my heart is overwhelmed; lead me to the rock that is higher than I. For You have been a shelter for me, a strong tower from the enemy. I will abide in Your tabernacle forever; I will trust in the shelter of Your wings. Selah. For You, O God, have heard my vows; You have given me the heritage of those who fear Your name. You will prolong the king's life, his years as many generations. He shall abide before God forever. Oh, prepare mercy and truth, which may preserve him! So I will sing praise to Your name forever, that I may daily perform my vows (Ps. 61:1-8, NKJ).

God took Shadrach, Meshach, and Abednego through the fiery furnace. God was with them in the fire:

Then King Nebuchadnezzar was astonished; and he rose in haste and spoke, saying to his counselors, "Did we not cast three men bound into the midst of the fire?" They answered and said to the king, "True, O king." "Look!" he answered, "I see four men loose, walking in the midst of the fire; and they are not hurt, and the form of the fourth is like the Son of God" (Dan. 3:24-25, NKJ).

Observe the glory that God received and the good experienced by Shadrach, Meshach, and Abednego after God took them through the fire:

Nebuchadnezzar spoke, saying, "Blessed be the God of Shadrach, Meshach, and Abed-Nego, who sent His Angel and delivered His servants who trusted in Him, and they have frustrated the king's word,

and yielded their bodies, that they should not serve nor worship any god except their own God! Therefore I make a decree that any people, nation, or language which speaks anything amiss against the God of Shadrach, Meshach, and Abed-Nego shall be cut in pieces, and their houses shall be made an ash heap; because there is no other God who can deliver like this." Then the king promoted Shadrach, Meshach, and Abed-Nego in the province of Babylon (Dan. 3:28-30, NKJ).

God took Daniel through the den of lions. Observe the glory that God received after taking Daniel through the lion's den:

Now the king went to his palace and spent the night fasting; and no musicians were brought before him. Also his sleep went from him. Then the king arose very early in the morning and went in haste to the den of lions. And when he came to the den, he cried out with a lamenting voice to Daniel. The king spoke, saying to Daniel, "Daniel, servant of the living God, has your God, whom you serve continually, been able to deliver you from the lions?" Then Daniel said to the king, "O king, live forever! My God sent His angel and shut the lions' mouths, so that they have not hurt me, because I was found innocent before Him; and also, O king, I have done no wrong before you." Then the king was exceedingly glad for him, and commanded that they should take Daniel up out of the den. So Daniel was taken up out of the den, and no injury whatever was found on him, because he believed in his God. And the king gave the command, and they brought those men who had accused Daniel, and they cast them into the den of lions - them, their children, and their wives; and the lions overpowered them, and broke all their bones in pieces before they ever came to the bottom of the den. Then King Darius wrote: "To all peoples, nations, and languages that dwell in all the earth: Peace be multiplied to you. I make a decree that in every dominion of my kingdom men must tremble and fear before the God of Daniel. For He is the living God, and steadfast forever; His kingdom is the one which shall not be destroyed, and His dominion shall endure to the end. He delivers and rescues, and He works signs and wonders in heaven and on earth, Who has delivered Daniel from the power of the lions" (Dan. 6:18-27, NKJ).

God takes us through some storms because going through them is sometimes necessary for God to accomplish His purposes in our lives.

Discussion Questions
Chapter 1

1. What words do you find comforting in Isaiah 43:1-3?

2. What passage or passages in the Bible have you found comforting during a storm in your life?

3. Who were some of the characters in the Bible that God took through storms?

4. How was God glorified after taking Daniel, Shadrach, Meshach, and Abednego through a storm?

5. What were some of the blessings received by Daniel, Shadrach, Meshach, and Abednego after God took them through a storm?

Reflections

1. Can you recall who or what helped you get through a storm in your life?

2. Can you recall some of the spiritual blessings you experienced after God took you through a storm?

Notes

Chapter 2

Storms to Disclose

The Bible teaches that God is omniscient, which means that God knows all there is to know about everyone and everything - past, present, and future (Ps. 139:1-3). Therefore, God is never surprised by what we say or do. However, we are sometimes surprised by what we say and do and what others say and do because we are not omniscient. Storms disclose both our strengths and our weaknesses to us and to others. God knows how we are going to respond because He is omniscient.

Satan caused the storm that killed the seven sons and three daughters of Job. However, Satan was not able to do anything to Job without God's permission (Job 1:12, 18-19). Satan accused Job of having a conditional faith (Job 1:9-11). The storm disclosed Job's genuine faith in God. Note the response of Job to the storm in his life:

While he was still speaking, another also came and said, "Your sons and daughters were eating and drinking wine in their oldest brother's house, and suddenly a great wind came from across the wilderness and struck the four corners of the house, and it fell on the young people, and they are dead; and I alone have escaped to tell you!" Then Job arose, tore his robe, and shaved his head; and he fell to the ground and worshiped. And he said: "Naked I came from my

mother's womb, and naked shall I return there. The LORD gave, and the LORD has taken away; blessed be the name of the Lord." In all this Job did not sin nor charge God with wrong (Job 1:18-22, NKJ).

Though He slay me, yet will I trust Him. Even so, I will defend my own ways before Him (Job 13:15, NKJ).

Satan did not expect Job to respond the way he did because Satan is not omniscient.

The Bible teaches that God is omnipotent, meaning that there are no limits to His power:

Is anything too hard for the Lord? At the appointed time I will return to you, according to the time of life, and Sarah shall have a son (Gen. 18:14, NKJ). Ah, Lord God! Behold, You have made the heavens and the earth by Your great power and outstretched arm. There is nothing too hard for You (Jer. 32:17, NKJ).

Satan has supernatural power, but he is not omnipotent. God has set limits on Satan's power:

And the Lord said to Satan, "Behold, all that he has is in your power; only do not lay a hand on his person." So Satan went out from the presence of the Lord (Job 1:12, NKJ).

Although Satan can go anywhere, he is not omnipresent:

Now there was a day when the sons of God came to present themselves before the Lord, and Satan also came among them. And the
Lord said to Satan, "From where do you come?" So Satan answered
the Lord and said, "From going to and fro on the earth, and from
walking back and forth on it" (Job 1:6-7, NKJ).

God, on the other hand, is everywhere at the same time:

Where can I go from Your Spirit? Or where can I flee from Your
presence? If I ascend into heaven, You are there; if I make my bed
in hell, behold, You are there. If I take the wings of the morning, and
dwell in the uttermost parts of the sea, even there Your hand shall
lead me, and Your right hand shall hold me. If I say, "Surely the
darkness shall fall on me," even the night shall be light about me;
indeed, the darkness shall not hide from You, but the night shines as
the day; the darkness and the light are both alike to You (Ps. 139:7-
12, NKJ).

The eyes of the Lord are in every place, keeping watch on the evil
and the good (Prov. 15:3, NKJ). "Can anyone hide himself in secret
places, so I shall not see him?" says the LORD; "Do I not fill heaven
and earth?" says the LORD (Jer. 23:24, NKJ).

And there is no creature hidden from His sight, but all things are
naked and open to the eyes of Him to whom we must give account
(Heb. 4:13, NKJ).

In Matthew 7:24-27, Jesus describes two builders. Both
builders appear to have built in the same location and to have

used the same building materials. However, one built his house upon a foundation of sand, but the other built his house upon a rock. It was a storm that disclosed the two foundations. Jesus points out that those who are obedient to His words are building their lives on a solid rock foundation, and they will be able to stand when the storms come. On the other hand, those who hear the words of Jesus but do not obey them are building on sand, and they will not be able to stand during the storms of life. The storms will disclose the foundation on which one has built:

Therefore whoever hears these sayings of Mine, and does them, I will liken him to a wise man who built his house on the rock: and the rain descended, the floods came, and the winds blew and beat on that house; and it did not fall, for it was founded on the rock. But everyone who hears these sayings of Mine, and does not do them, will be like a foolish man who built his house on the sand: and the rain descended, the floods came, and the winds blew and beat on that house; and it fell. And great was its fall (Matt. 7:24-27, NKJ).

The storm recorded in Mark 4:35-41 disclosed both the humanity and the divinity of Jesus Christ. The humanity of Jesus was seen in the fact that He was sleeping in a great storm, and He had to be awakened by His disciples:

And a great windstorm arose, and the waves beat into the boat, so

that it was already filling. But He was in the stern, asleep on a pillow. And they awoke Him and said to Him, "Teacher, do You not care that we are perishing?" (Mark 4:37-38, NKJ).

The divinity of Jesus was disclosed when He spoke and immediately the storm ceased:

Then He arose and rebuked the wind, and said to the sea, "Peace, be still!" And the wind ceased and there was a great calm. But He said to them, "Why are you so fearful? How is it that you have no faith?" And they feared exceedingly, and said to one another, "Who can this be, that even the wind and the sea obey Him!" (Mark 4:39-41, NKJ).

I believe that the disciples awoke Jesus because they wanted Him to help them to get water out of their boat. Notice again Mark 4:37-38:

And a great windstorm arose, and the waves beat into the boat, so that it was already filling. But He was in the stern, asleep on a pillow. And they awoke Him and said to Him, "Teacher, do You not care that we are perishing?"

I do not believe that the disciples were expecting Jesus to speak and still the storm. The disciples feared the storm, but after Jesus stilled the storm, they feared Him more than they had feared the storm because they recognized that God was in their boat. Observe the reaction of the disciples to the stilling of the storm in Mark 4:39-41:

Then He arose and rebuked the wind, and said to the sea, "Peace, be still!" And the wind ceased and there was a great calm. But He said to them, "Why are you so fearful? How is it that you have no faith?" And they feared exceedingly, and said to one another, "Who can this be, that even the wind and the sea obey Him!"

The storm disclosed both the humanity and the divinity of Jesus Christ.

God may use a storm to disclose us to ourselves. God knows all there is to know about us. God knows how we are going to respond to storms. However, there is a lot about ourselves that we do not know. During the storms we learn a lot about ourselves. We discover how strong or weak our faith is in God. We learn about our patience, our prayer life, our perseverance, and so on.

God may use a storm to disclose us to others. Someone may come to faith in God and some may find encouragement by observing how God takes us through a storm.

God may use storms to disclose others to us. Storms disclose who your friends really are. Storms also disclose those in your family and fellowship on whom you can depend when you need help.

God may also use a storm to disclose Himself to us. Notice the words of Job after he had gone through a storm:

I have heard of You by the hearing of the ear, but now my eye sees You. Therefore I abhor myself, and repent in dust and ashes (Job 42:5-6, NKJ).

Discussion Questions
Chapter 2

1. What were some of the things that Satan was able to do to Job with God's permission?

2. How does Jesus teach us to prepare for storms?

3. How did the storm in Job's life disclose his faith?

4. Why did God permit Satan to attack Job?

Reflections

1. Can you recall a storm in which disclosures were made regarding yourself, others, or God?

2. What has a storm disclosed to you about yourself?

3. What have storms disclosed to you about others?

4. What have storms disclosed to you about God?

Notes

Chapter 3

Storms to Develop

After feeding over five thousand with two fish and five loaves of bread, Jesus persuaded His disciples to get into a boat and go across the Sea of Galilee to Bethsaida while He sent the multitude away (Mark 6:44-45). Having sent the disciples and the multitude away, Jesus went up into a mountain to pray (Mark 6:46). The disciples encountered a storm in the middle of the Sea of Galilee:

Now when evening came, the boat was in the middle of the sea; and He was alone on the land. Then He saw them straining at rowing, for the wind was against them. Now about the fourth watch of the night He came to them, walking on the sea, and would have passed them by (Mark 6:47-48, NKJ).

Jesus knew that the disciples were going to encounter this storm, and He saw them struggling in the storm. I believe that Jesus wanted to develop faith and perseverance in His disciples. Jesus wants to develop faith in all of His followers because we walk by faith and not by sight (2 Cor. 5:7), and without faith it is impossible to please God (Heb. 11:6).

Storms may be permitted to develop faith and other Christ-like qualities in believers in Christ. For example, a thorn was permitted in Paul's life to develop humility:

And lest I should be exalted above measure by the abundance of the revelations, a thorn in the flesh was given to me, a messenger of Satan to buffet me, lest I be exalted above measure. Concerning this thing I pleaded with the Lord three times that it might depart from me. And He said to me, "My grace is sufficient for you, for My strength is made perfect in weakness." Therefore most gladly I will rather boast in my infirmities, that the power of Christ may rest upon me. Therefore I take pleasure in infirmities, in reproaches, in needs, in persecutions, in distresses, for Christ's sake. For when I am weak, then I am strong (2 Cor. 2:7-10, NKJ).

The Bible teaches that God may use storms to develop patience or endurance or perseverance or other Christ-like qualities in us:

And not only that, but we also glory in tribulations, knowing that tribulation produces perseverance (Rom. 5:3, NKJ).

My brethren, count it all joy when you fall into various trials, knowing that the testing of your faith produces patience. But let patience have its perfect work, that you may be perfect and complete, lacking nothing (James 1:2-4, NKJ).

But may the God of all grace, who called us to His eternal glory by

Christ Jesus, after you have suffered a while, perfect, establish, strengthen, and settle you (1 Pet. 5:10, NKJ).

God may use storms to develop us into those who will be comforters to others:

Blessed be the God and Father of our Lord Jesus Christ, the Father of mercies and God of all comfort, who comforts us in all our tribulation, that we may be able to comfort those who are in any trouble, with the comfort with which we ourselves are comforted by God (2 Cor. 1:3-4, NKJ).

Observe that the disciples were in a storm because of their obedience to Jesus. Sometimes we are in storms because we have obeyed the Word of God and are in the will of God. Storms do not always mean that one is out of the will of God.

Notice that while Jesus was praying, He saw His disciples struggling in the storm:

Then He saw them straining at rowing, for the wind was against them. Now about the fourth watch of the night He came to them, walking on the sea, and would have passed them by (Mark 6:48, NKJ).

Jesus sees us when we are in storms, and the Bible teaches that He is praying for us (Rom. 8:34; Heb. 7:25, NKJ).

Observe that in obedience to Jesus, the disciples continued

to struggle in the storm even though they were not making any progress (Mark 6:48). The wind was against the disciples. Therefore, if they had turned back, the wind would have conveyed them back to their starting point without any effort. The disciples persevered because Jesus promised to meet them on the other side of the Sea of Galilee. When you are in a storm because of your obedience to the Word of God, continue to obey even though you may not seem to be making any progress. Continue to stand on the promises of God. Jesus eventually came to the disciples in the storm walking on the sea between 3:00 a.m. and 6:00 a.m. Although Jesus sees us struggling in the storm, He may not come immediately with deliverance because there are Christ-like qualities that He wants to develop in us.

Discussion Questions
Chapter 3

1. Why did Jesus send His disciples into a storm?

2. Why did the disciples of Jesus persevere in a storm when they were not making progress?

3. Why did Jesus wait until the fourth watch of the night before going to His disciples?

4. What Christ-like qualities did the storm develop in the disciples?

Reflections

1. Can you recall a storm that you experienced because of your obedience to the Word of God?

2. Can you identify a Christ-like quality that was developed as a result of going through a storm?

Notes

Chapter 4

Storms to Discipline

The Bible teaches that God is a loving Father who disciplines His children because of love and concern for them. Note the following Scriptures:

You should know in your heart that as a man chastens his son, so the LORD your God chastens you (Deut. 8:5, NKJ).

Behold, happy is the man whom God corrects; therefore do not despise the chastening of the Almighty (Job 5:17, NKJ).

My son, do not despise the chastening of the LORD, nor detest His correction; for whom the Lord loves He corrects, just as a father the son in whom he delights (Prov. 3:11-12, NKJ).

And you have forgotten the exhortation which speaks to you as to sons: "My son, do not despise the chastening of the LORD, nor be discouraged when you are rebuked by Him; for whom the LORD loves He chastens, and scourges every son whom He receives." If you endure chastening, God deals with you as with sons; for what son is there whom a father does not chasten? But if you are without chastening, of which all have become partakers, then you are illegitimate and not sons. Furthermore, we have had human fathers who corrected us, and we paid them respect. Shall we not much more readily be in subjection to the Father of spirits and live? For they indeed for a

few days chastened us as seemed best to them, but He for our profit, that we may be partakers of His holiness. Now no chastening seems to be joyful for the present, but painful; nevertheless, afterward it yields the peaceable fruit of righteousness to those who have been trained by it (Heb. 12:5-11, NKJ).

The storm in the Book of Jonah was produced by God to discipline Jonah. God commanded Jonah to go to Nineveh and preach a message of judgment. However, Jonah went in the opposite direction to Tarshish because the Ninevites were enemies of the Hebrews, and Jonah did not want God to spare them. Jonah knew that if the people of Nineveh repented, God would be gracious to them. Note the anger and displeasure of Jonah after the repentance of the Ninevites:

But it displeased Jonah exceedingly, and he became angry. So he prayed to the Lord, and said, "Ah, Lord, was not this what I said when I was still in my country? Therefore I fled previously to Tarshish; for I know that You are a gracious and merciful God, slow to anger and abundant in lovingkindness, One who relents from doing harm. "Therefore now, O Lord, please take my life from me, for it is better for me to die than to live!" (Jonah 4:1-3, NKJ).

God may use a storm as an instrument of discipline when His children disobey His Word and get out of His will:

Now the word of the Lord came to Jonah the son of Amittai,

saying, "Arise, go to Nineveh, that great city, and cry out against it;
for their wickedness has come up before Me." But Jonah arose to
flee to Tarshish from the presence of the Lord. He went down to
Joppa, and found a ship going to Tarshish; so he paid the fare, and
went down into it, to go with them to Tarshish from the presence of
the Lord. But the Lord sent out a great wind on the sea, and there
was a mighty tempest on the sea, so that the ship was about to be
broken up (Jonah 1:1-4, NKJ).

We have seen that the disciples were in a storm because of
their obedience to Jesus (Mark 6:45-48). In contrast, Jonah
was in a storm because of His disobedience to God. Hence, the
storm in the life of Jonah could have been avoided if Jonah
had obeyed God. We bring some storms on ourselves because
of our disobedience. It is interesting to note that everything in
the Book of Jonah obeyed God except Jonah. The wind obeyed
God (Jonah 1:4; 4:8); the whale or great fish obeyed God
(Jonah 1:17; 2:10); the weed obeyed God (Jonah 4:6); the
worm obeyed God (Jonah 4:7). Jonah, on the other hand, did
not obey God until after the storm and big fish experience.
Note that what God said to Jonah in chapter 1:1-2, He repeated
in chapter 3:1-2. The chapter 2 experiences involving the big
fish could have been avoided. God's Word will not change.
God will not change nor modify His Word to please us. These
Words will not change:

Therefore if you bring your gift to the altar, and there remember that your brother has something against you, leave your gift there before the altar, and go your way. First be reconciled to your brother, and then come and offer your gift (Matt. 5:23-24, NKJ).

You have heard that it was said, "You shall love your neighbor and hate your enemy." But I say to you, love your enemies, bless those who curse you, do good to those who hate you, and pray for those who spitefully use you and persecute you, that you may be sons of your Father in heaven; for He makes His sun rise on the evil and on the good, and sends rain on the just and on the unjust (Matt. 5:43-45, NKJ).

But seek first the kingdom of God and His righteousness, and all these things shall be added to you (Matt. 6:33, NKJ).

Moreover if your brother sins against you, go and tell him his fault between you and him alone. If he hears you, you have gained your brother. But if he will not hear, take with you one or two more, that by the mouth of two or three witnesses every word may be established. And if he refuses to hear them, tell it to the church. But if he refuses even to hear the church, let him be to you like a heathen and a tax collector (Matt. 18:15-17, NKJ).

Jesus answered and said to him, "Most assuredly, I say to you, unless one is born again, he cannot see the kingdom of God" (John 3:3, NKJ).

He who believes in the Son has everlasting life; and he who does not believe the Son shall not see life, but the wrath of God abides on him (John

3:36, NKJ).

Most assuredly, I say to you, he who hears My word and believes in Him who sent Me has everlasting life, and shall not come into judgment, but has passed from death into life (John 5:24, NKJ).

Jesus said to him, "I am the way, the truth, and the life. No one comes to the Father except through Me" (John 14:6, NKJ).

Beloved, do not avenge yourselves, but rather give place to wrath; for it is written, "Vengeance is Mine, I will repay," says the Lord (Rom. 12:19, NKJ).

Do not be deceived, God is not mocked; for whatever a man sows, that he will also reap (Gal. 6:7, NKJ).

Discussion Question
Chapter 4

1. Why did Jonah disobey the command of God to go to Nineveh?

2. What were some of the experiences that Jonah could have avoided if he had obeyed God?

3. Why did God discipline Jonah?

Reflections

1. Can you recall a storm that you experienced because of your disobedience to God?

2. Can you recall the lessons that you learned from the storm?

Notes

Chapter 5

Storms to Direct

The storm in the Book of Jonah was sent by God not only to discipline Jonah but also to direct him to Nineveh:

Now the word of the LORD came to Jonah the son of Amittai, saying, "Arise, go to Nineveh, that great city, and cry out against it; for their wickedness has come up before Me." But Jonah arose to flee to Tarshish from the presence of the LORD. He went down to Joppa, and found a ship going to Tarshish; so he paid the fare, and went down into it, to go with them to Tarshish from the presence of the LORD. But the LORD sent out a great wind on the sea, and there was a mighty tempest on the sea, so that the ship was about to be broken up (Jonah 1:1-4, NKJ).

The sailors eventually threw Jonah into the sea because of the storm that was sent by God:

Then they said to him, "What shall we do to you that the sea may be calm for us?" - for the sea was growing more tempestuous. And he said to them, "Pick me up and throw me into the sea; then the sea will become calm for you. For I know that this great tempest is because of me." Nevertheless the men rowed hard to return to land, but they could not, for the sea continued to grow more tempestuous against them. Therefore they cried out to the LORD and said, "We pray, O LORD, please do not let us perish for this man's life, and

do not charge us with innocent blood; for You, O LORD, have done as it pleased You." So they picked up Jonah and threw him into the sea, and the sea ceased from its raging (Jonah 1:11-15, NKJ).

God prepared a fish to swallow Jonah and to transport him to Nineveh:

Now the LORD had prepared a great fish to swallow Jonah. And Jonah was in the belly of the fish three days and three nights. So the LORD spoke to the fish, and it vomited Jonah onto dry land (Jonah 1:17; 2:10, NKJ).

God may permit or produce storms in our lives to direct us from point A to point B. For example, God permitted Joseph to be sold into slavery by his brothers because God wanted Joseph in Egypt. Joseph was in Egypt for about thirteen years before he understood why God had directed him there. Note what Joseph later said to his brothers:

And Joseph said to his brothers, "Please come near to me." So they came near. Then he said: "I am Joseph your brother, whom you sold into Egypt. But now, do not therefore be grieved or angry with your-selves because you sold me here; for God sent me before you to pre-serve life. For these two years the famine has been in the land, and there are still five years in which there will be neither plowing nor harvesting. And God sent me before you to preserve a posterity for you in the earth, and to save your lives by a great deliverance. So now it was not you who sent me here, but God; and He has made

me a father to Pharaoh, and lord of all his house, and a ruler throughout all the land of Egypt" (Gen. 45:4-8, NKJ). But as for you, you meant evil against me; but God meant it for good, in order to bring it about as it is this day, to save many people alive (Gen. 50:20, NKJ).

God's plan was to develop the nation of Israel in Egypt:

Then God spoke to Israel in the visions of the night, and said, "Jacob, Jacob!" And he said, "Here I am." So He said, "I am God, the God of your father; do not fear to go down to Egypt, for I will make of you a great nation there. I will go down with you to Egypt, and I will also surely bring you up again; and Joseph will put his hand on your eyes" (Gen. 46:2-4, NKJ).

God used a famine to get Joseph's family to move to Egypt. When Joseph interpreted Pharaoh's dream, he pointed out that God was going to cause a famine: "This is the thing which I have spoken to Pharaoh. God has shown Pharaoh what He is about to do" (Gen. 41:28, NKJ).

Joseph's brothers went to Egypt to buy food and the family later moved there because of the famine:

When Jacob saw that there was grain in Egypt, Jacob said to his sons, "Why do you look at one another?" And he said, "Indeed I have heard that there is grain in Egypt; go down to that place and buy for us there, that we may live and not die."

So Joseph's ten brothers went down to buy grain in Egypt (Gen. 42:1-3, NKJ).

Hurry and go up to my father, and say to him, "Thus says your son Joseph: God has made me lord of all Egypt; come down to me, do not tarry. You shall dwell in the land of Goshen, and you shall be near to me, you and your children, your children's children, your flocks and your herds, and all that you have. There I will provide for you, lest you and your household, and all that you have, come to poverty; for there are still five years of famine" (Gen. 45:9-11, NKJ).

In the Book of Acts, we see another example of God using a storm to direct His people from point A to point B. In Acts 1:8, Jesus commanded His followers to witness in Jerusalem, in all Judea and Samaria and to the end of the earth. Many of the followers of Christ remained in Jerusalem until the storm of persecution moved them throughout the region of Judea and Samaria: "But you shall receive power when the Holy Spirit has come upon you; and you shall be witnesses to Me in Jerusalem, and in all Judea and Samaria, and to the end of the earth" (Acts 1:8, NKJ). "Now Saul was consenting to his death. At that time a great persecution arose against the church which was at Jerusalem; and they were all scattered throughout the regions of Judea and Samaria, except the apostles" (Acts 8:1, NKJ).

For over twenty-seven years, I have been a pastor in the City of Milwaukee. I believe that I am where God wants me at the present time. It was the loss of a job in Memphis, Tennessee, in February, 1960, that led me to move to Milwaukee. As I now look back, I thank God for the storm that moved me from Memphis to Milwaukee.

Discussion Questions
Chapter 5

1. How long was Joseph in the dark regarding why he was in Egypt?

2. What storms did God use to get Joseph and his family in Egypt?

3. Why did God want Joseph and his family in Egypt?

4. Why was Joseph forgiving toward his brothers who sold him into slavery?

Reflections:

1. Can you recall a storm that God used to direct you from point A to point B?

2. How long were you in the dark before you understood what God was doing?

Notes

Chapter 6

Storms to Draw

Jesus said that no one could come to Him unless drawn by God the Father: "No one can come to Me unless the Father who sent Me draws him; and I will raise him up at the last day" (John 6:44, NKJ). According to Jeremiah 31:3, God draws us because of His love for us:

The LORD has appeared of old to me, saying: "Yes, I have loved you with an everlasting love; therefore with lovingkindness I have drawn you."

God uses many instruments to draw people to Himself both in salvation and in service. One of God's instruments is a storm. I believe that God used the storm recorded in Acts 27 to draw many to Himself in salvation.

We learn from Acts 27 that Paul was a prisoner who was being taken on a ship to Rome to be tried. According to Acts 27:37, there were 276 passengers on the ship including Paul and Luke, the writer. Most of the passengers were prisoners. I believe that Paul prayed for the salvation of all of the lost souls on the ship. I also believe that many were drawn to

Christ as a result of the storm that occurred. Note the promise of God to Paul through an angel:

And now I urge you to take heart, for there will be no loss of life among you, but only of the ship. For there stood by me this night an angel of the God to whom I belong and whom I serve, saying, "Do not be afraid, Paul; you must be brought before Caesar; and indeed God has granted you all those who sail with you." Therefore take heart, men, for I believe God that it will be just as it was told me (Acts 27:22-25, NKJ).

Observe that the storm in Acts 27 could have been avoided if the advice of Paul, the man of God, had been followed. Paul warned the officer in charge of the prisoners not to continue the voyage because the dangerous season for sailing had begun. However, the officer listened to the majority and continued the voyage to Rome. It was not long after continuing that a storm was encountered (Acts 27:9-15). Although Paul was not a professional sailor, he was an experienced traveler who knew a few things about storms and shipwrecks: "Three times I was beaten with rods; once I was stoned; three times I was shipwrecked; a night and a day I have been in the deep" (2 Cor. 11:25, NKJ).

In chapter 3, we saw the disciples of Jesus in a storm because of their obedience to Christ. In chapter 4, we saw

Jonah in a storm because of disobedience to God. In Acts 27, we see Paul in a storm because of the disobedience of someone else. Perhaps one of the worst types of storm is the one that you tried to avoid, but you are in it because your advice or warning was not followed or because of someone else's disobedience to the Word of God. Sometimes we are in storms because we are on board a ship with a relative, friend, or coworker who has disobeyed the Word of God; and therefore is out of the will of God.

Observe that when we pray for someone to be saved, God may use a storm to draw them to Jesus; and we may be on board with them when the storm comes. Remember that you may be in a storm because God is simply answering a prayer that you have prayed. For example, one day the Brook Cherith dried up for Elijah because he had prayed for God to shut up the heavens and withhold the rain (1 Kings 17:7; cf. James 5:17).

In the Gospels, we see many drawn to Jesus because of figurative storms in their lives. For example, the Syrophenician woman was drawn to Jesus because of a demon in the life of her daughter (Matt. 15:21-28; Mark 7:24-30). The woman with the issue of blood for twelve years was drawn to Jesus because she had spent all of her money on doctors and her condition had not improved (Matt. 9:20-22; Mark 5:25-34; Luke 8:43-

48). There was a leper who came to Jesus because of his disease (Matt. 8:1-3). Jairus came to Jesus because of the condition of his daughter (Mark 5:22-24). Blind Bartimaeus came to Jesus because of his blindness (Mark 10:46-52).

God may use a literal or a figurative storm to draw His people back to Him once they have wandered away. In Amos 4:6-11, NKJ, God takes responsibility for the figurative storms mentioned, and God points out that He sent the storms to draw His people back to Himself. Note the refrain, "Yet you have not returned to Me":

Also I gave you cleanness of teeth in all your cities. And lack of bread in all your places; Yet you have not returned to Me, Says the LORD. I also withheld rain from you, when there were still three months to the harvest. I made it rain on one city, I withheld rain from another city. One part was rained upon, and where it did not rain the part withered. So two or three cities wandered to another city to drink water, but they were not satisfied; Yet you have not returned to Me, Says the LORD. I blasted you with blight and mildew. When your gardens increased, your vineyards, your fig trees, and your olive trees, the locust devoured them; Yet you have not returned to Me, Says the LORD. I sent among you a plague after the manner of Egypt; Your young men I killed with a sword, along with your captive horses; I made the stench of your camps come up into your nostrils; Yet you have not returned to Me, Says the LORD. I overthrew some of you, as God overthrew Sodom and Gomorrah, and you were like a firebrand plucked from the burning; Yet you have not returned to Me, Says the LORD.

Observe that the storms increased because God's people did not recognize their sins, repent, and return to God. Here the storms would have ceased if God's people had simply recognized their sins, repented of their sins, and returned to God.

Isaiah points out that we are all like sheep. We tend to go our own way:

All we like sheep have gone astray; we have turned, every one, to his own way; and the LORD has laid on Him the iniquity of us all (Isa. 53:6, NKJ).

Our proneness to wander is also pointed out in the Hymn "Come Thou Fount" by Robert Robinson:

O to grace how great a debtor Daily I'm constrained to be!
Let Thy goodness, like a fetter, Bind my wandering heart to Thee:
Prone to wander, Lord, I feel it, Prone to leave the God I love;
Here's my heart, O take and seal it; Seal it for Thy courts above.

Discussion Questions
Chapter 6

1. Why was the advice of Paul not followed?

2. Why should the advice of Paul have been followed?

Reflections

1. Can you recall a storm that you were in because you were close to someone who was disobedient to the Word of God and therefore was out of the will of God?

2. Can you recall a storm that you were in because someone did not follow your advice or warning?

3. Can you recall a storm that you experienced because you did not follow godly advice?

4. Can you recall a storm that drew you closer to God?

Notes

Chapter 7

How to Go Through
a Storm

On the voyage of life, we are all either headed for a storm; or we are in a storm; or we have come out of a storm. When we are in a storm, the way out of the storm is through the storm. Since no one is exempt from storms, it is important that we learn how to go through them God's way. We can learn from Job and other biblical characters how to go through a storm.

CONTINUE TO PRAY

In the context of trials, James exhorts us to pray for wisdom: "If any of you lacks wisdom, let him ask of God, who gives to all liberally and without reproach, and it will be given to him" (James 1:5, NKJ). "Wisdom" is a translation of the Greek word "sophia." One of the meanings of "sophia" is the right use of knowledge. Pray for wisdom to apply what you know about trials. Pray for wisdom not to waste the trial or storm.

Pray also for grace. James mentions falling into "various

trials": "My brethren, count it all joy when you fall into "various trials" (James 1:2, NKJ). The adjective "various" is a translation of the Greek word "poikílos," which means "many colored." Peter uses the same adjective, "poikílos," to describe the grace of God: "As each one has received a gift, minister it to one another, as good stewards of the manifold [poikilos] grace of God" (1 Pet. 4:10, NKJ). Trials come in many different colors, but God has the same color of grace to match each trial. God's grace is sufficient (2 Cor. 12:9). There is an abundant supply of God's grace (John 1:16; Rom. 5:20; 1 Tim. 1:14).

We are invited to come to the throne of grace (Heb. 4:16). The Bible speaks of saving grace (Eph. 2:8-9), serving grace (Heb. 12:28), shaping grace (1 Cor. 15:10), sharing grace (2 Cor. 8:1-2, 7), strengthening grace (Acts 20:32; 2 Tim. 2:1), speaking grace (Eph. 4:29; Col. 4:6; Rom. 12:3), singing grace (Col. 3:16), stopping or restraining grace (Gen. 20:6; 31:7; 35:5; 1 Sam. 25:26, 34), and suffering grace (2 Cor. 12:9).

CONTINUE TO PRAISE AND WORSHIP GOD

Job continued to praise and worship God in the midst of the worst storm in his life:

Then Job arose, tore his robe, and shaved his head; and he fell to the

ground and worshiped. And he said: "Naked I came from my mother's womb, and naked shall I return there. The Lord gave, and the Lord has taken away; blessed be the name of the Lord." In all this Job did not sin nor charge God with wrong (Job 1:20-22, NKJ).

Job was obedient to the first and great commandment, which is to love God more than anything and anyone on the earth:

Hear, O Israel: The LORD our God, the LORD is one! You shall love the Lord your God with all your heart, with all your soul, and with all your strength (Deut. 6:4-5, NKJ).

Then one of them, a lawyer, asked Him a question, testing Him, and saying, "Teacher, which is the great commandment in the law? " Jesus said to him, "You shall love the Lord your God with all your heart, with all your soul, and with all your mind. This is the first and great commandment" (Matt. 22:35-38, NKJ).

When Job lost all of his material possessions, he still had what he loved and valued most - God!

David also continued to worship God after the loss of his son by Bathsheba, even though he prayed and fasted for God to spare the child's life:

When David saw that his servants were whispering, David perceived

that the child was dead. Therefore David said to his servants, "Is the child dead?" And they said, "He is dead." So David arose from the ground, washed and anointed himself, and changed his clothes; and he went into the house of the Lord and worshiped. Then he went to his own house; and when he requested, they set food before him, and he ate (2 Sam. 12:19-20, NKJ).

David was sincere when he wrote: I will bless the Lord at all times; His praise shall continually be in my mouth (Ps. 34:1, NKJ).

Habakkuk vowed to continue to praise and worship God in the midst of the storm in his life. He said:

Though the fig tree may not blossom, nor fruit be on the vines; though the labor of the olive may fail, and the fields yield no food; though the flock may be cut off from the fold, and there be no herd in the stalls. Yet I will rejoice in the LORD, I will joy in the God of my salvation. The LORD God is my strength; He will make my feet like deer's feet, and He will make me walk on my high hills (Hab. 3:17-19, NKJ).

Paul and Silas were heard praying and praising God at midnight in the midst of their storm: "But at midnight Paul and Silas were praying and singing hymns to God, and the prisoners were listening to them" (Acts 16:25, NKJ). To praise and worship at midnight, one must practice in the daylight before midnight comes.

CONTINUE TO RECOGNIZE AND REST IN THE SOVEREIGNTY OF GOD

The sovereignty of God means that God does what He wills, when He wills, where He wills, how He wills, and with whom He wills. The following are some passages in the Bible that refer to the sovereignty of God:

Whatever the LORD pleases He does, in heaven and in earth, in the seas and in all deep places (Ps. 135:6, NKJ).

Remember the former things of old, for I am God, and there is no other; I am God, and there is none like Me, declaring the end from the beginning, and from ancient times things that are not yet done, Saying, "My counsel shall stand, and I will do all My pleasure" (Isa. 46:9-10, NKJ).

All the inhabitants of the earth are reputed as nothing; He does according to His will in the army of heaven and among the inhabitants of the earth. No one can restrain His hand or say to Him, "What have You done?" (Daniel 4:35, NKJ).

Men of Israel, hear these words: Jesus of Nazareth, a Man attested by God to you by miracles, wonders, and signs which God did through Him in your midst, as you yourselves also know - Him, being delivered by the determined purpose and foreknowledge of God, you have taken by lawless hands, have crucified, and put to death (Acts 2:22-23, NKJ).

And being let go, they went to their own companions and reported all that the chief priests and elders had said to them. So when they heard that, they raised their voice to God with one accord and said: "Lord, You are God, who made heaven and earth and the sea, and all that is in them, who by the mouth of Your servant David have said: 'Why did the nations rage, and the people plot vain things? The kings of the earth took their stand, and the rulers were gathered together against the Lord and against His Christ.' For truly against Your holy Servant Jesus, whom You anointed, both Herod and Pontius Pilate, with the Gentiles and the people of Israel, were gathered together to do whatever Your hand and Your purpose determined before to be done" (Acts 4:23-28, NKJ).

For He says to Moses, "I will have mercy on whomever I will have mercy, and I will have compassion on whomever I will have compassion." So then it is not of him who wills, nor of him who runs, but of God who shows mercy. For the Scripture says to Pharaoh, "For this very purpose I have raised you up, that I may show My power in you, and that My name may be declared in all the earth." Therefore He has mercy on whom He wills, and whom He wills He hardens (Romans 9:15-18, NKJ).

Notice Job's recognition of God's sovereignty:

Then Job arose, tore his robe, and shaved his head; and he fell to the ground and worshiped. And he said: "Naked I came from my mother's womb, and naked shall I return there. The LORD gave, and the

LORD has taken away; blessed be the name of the LORD." In all this Job did not sin nor charge God with wrong (Job 1:20-22, NKJ).

Then his wife said to him, "Do you still hold fast to your integrity? Curse God and die!" But he said to her, "You speak as one of the foolish women speaks. Shall we indeed accept good from God, and shall we not accept adversity?" In all this Job did not sin with his lips (Job 2:9-10, NKJ).

If He takes away, who can hinder Him? Who can say to Him, "What are You doing?" (Job 9:12, NKJ).

But He is unique, and who can make Him change? And whatever His soul desires, that He does. For He performs what is appointed for me, and many such things are with Him. (Job 23:13-14, NKJ).

He stretches out the north over empty space; He hangs the earth on nothing (Job 26:7, NKJ).

CONTINUE TO TRUST GOD

Job continued to trust God throughout the storms in his life. Job said, "Though He slay me, yet will I trust Him" (Job 13:15a, NKJ). David, Daniel, Shadrach, Meshach, Abednego, Peter, Paul, and many other saints continued to trust God during storms in their lives. Paul points out in 2 Corinthians 5:7 that "We walk by faith, not by sight." The writer of Hebrews reminds us "without faith it is impossible to please God"

(Heb. 11:6). We are commanded in Proverbs to "Trust in the LORD with all your heart, and lean not on your own understanding; in all your ways acknowledge Him, and He shall direct your paths" (Prov. 3:5-6, NKJ).

CONTINUE TO WAIT FOR YOUR CHANGE

In Isaiah 40:31, there is a beautiful promise: "But those who wait on the LORD shall renew their strength; they shall mount up with wings like eagles, they shall run and not be weary, they shall walk and not faint."

In the midst of the storm in his life, Job said, "All the days of my hard service I will wait, till my change comes" (Job 14:14b, NKJ). Note the change that came for Job at the end of the Book of Job:

And the LORD restored Job's losses when he prayed for his friends. Indeed the LORD gave Job twice as much as he had before. Then all his brothers, all his sisters, and all those who had been his acquaintances before, came to him and ate food with him in his house; and they consoled him and comforted him for all the adversity that the LORD had brought upon him. Each one gave him a piece of silver and each a ring of gold. Now the LORD blessed the latter days of Job more than his beginning; for he had fourteen thousand sheep, six thousand camels, one thousand yoke of oxen, and one thousand female donkeys. He also had seven sons and three daughters. And he called the name of the first Jemimah, the name of the second Keziah, and the name of the third Keren-Happuch. In all the land were

found no women so beautiful as the daughters of Job; and their father gave them an inheritance among their brothers. After this Job lived one hundred and forty years, and saw his children and grand-children for four generations. So Job died, old and full of days (Job 42:10-17, NKJ).

The question is "How long must I wait?" The wait may be a short time. Psalm 30:5b says, "Weeping may endure for a night, but joy comes in the morning." The wait may be a long period of time. Joseph waited for thirteen years before his change came (cf. Gen. 37:2; 41:46). Storms eventually end. The clouds will disappear, and the sun will shine again. The change may be grace. God did not remove the thorn in Paul's life, but God did give Paul the necessary grace to bear it (2 Cor. 12:7-10).

CONTINUE TO STAND ON WHAT YOU KNOW

Job did not know why he lost his ten children, all of his material possessions, and his health. However, Job said that he knew that his redeemer lived:

For I know that my Redeemer lives, and He shall stand at last on the earth; and after my skin is destroyed, this I know, that in my flesh I shall see God, Whom I shall see for myself, and my eyes shall behold, and not another. How my heart yearns within me! (Job 19:25-27, NKJ).

When you have a situation that you do not understand, recall, reflect, and rest on what you do understand. Stand on what you know. For example, I know that I am a child of the King. I know that God is sovereign. I know that Satan cannot make a move against me without God's permission. I know that God arranges things. I know that God is able to work all things together for the good of those who love Him and are called according to His purposes. I know that God has all wisdom and knowledge and that He does not make mistakes. God has all power. God knows everything. God is everywhere. Stand on what you know!

When you are in a storm, it is also helpful to find a promise, state it, and stand on it. Note how Paul stated and stood on a promise that God gave to him in a storm:

And now I urge you to take heart, for there will be no loss of life among you, but only of the ship. For there stood by me this night an angel of the God to whom I belong and whom I serve, saying, "Do not be afraid, Paul; you must be brought before Caesar; and indeed God has granted you all those who sail with you." Therefore take heart, men, for I believe God that it will be just as it was told me (Acts 27:22-25, NKJ).

CONTINUE TO PERSEVERE
The disciples of Jesus continued to persevere after they

encountered a storm on the Sea of Galilee. Jesus was praying while His disciples were struggling in the storm:

Immediately He made His disciples get into the boat and go before Him to the other side, to Bethsaida, while He sent the multitude away. And when He had sent them away, He departed to the mountain to pray. Now when evening came, the boat was in the middle of the sea; and He was alone on the land. Then He saw them straining at rowing, for the wind was against them. Now about the fourth watch of the night He came to them, walking on the sea, and would have passed them by (Mark 6:45-48, NKJ).

The disciples of Jesus persevered because Jesus commanded them to go to the other side of the Sea of Galilee to Bethsaida.

CONTINUE TO LOOK BEYOND THE PROCESS TO THE PRODUCT

Storms are processes that God uses to produce products. Job said, "But He knows the way that I take; When He has tested me, I shall come forth as gold" (Job 23:10, NKJ).

James tells us to "count it all joy when you fall into various trials" (James 1:2, NKJ). James points out four products of the process: endurance, spiritual maturity, wholeness, and no deficiencies: "knowing that the testing of your faith produces patience. But let patience have its perfect work, that you may be perfect and complete, lacking nothing" (James 1:3-4, NKJ).

Peter also points out four products of the process of storms: "But may the God of all grace, who called us to His eternal glory by Christ Jesus, after you have suffered a while, perfect, establish, strengthen, and settle you" (1 Pet. 5:10, NKJ).

According to Hebrews 12:2, Jesus endured the cross because of what He saw beyond the cross. Jesus looked beyond the process to the products: One of the products that Jesus saw beyond the process was His seat at the right hand of the Father (Isa. 52:13; Heb. 12:2; 1:3; 8:1). There was no seat in the Tabernacle nor was there a seat later in the Temple because the work of the High Priest was never done. However, when Jesus died on the cross, the work of redemption was finished once and for all:

In burnt offerings and sacrifices for sin You had no pleasure. Then I said, "Behold, I have come In the volume of the book it is written of Me To do Your will, O God." Previously saying, "Sacrifice and offering, burnt offerings, and offerings for sin You did not desire, nor had pleasure in them" (which are offered according to the law), then He said, "Behold, I have come to do Your will, O God." He takes away the first that He may establish the second. By that will we have been sanctified through the offering of the body of Jesus Christ once for all. And every priest stands ministering daily and offering repeatedly the same sacrifices, which can never take away sins. But this Man, after He had offered one sacrifice for sins forever, sat down at the

right hand of God (Heb. 10:6-12, NKJ).

So when Jesus had received the sour wine, He said, "It is finished!" And bowing His head, He gave up His spirit (John 19:30, NKJ).

Because the work of redemption is now completed, Jesus is now in the place of honor in His glorified body seated at the right hand of God the Father interceding for us (Rom. 8:34; Heb. 7:25).

The second product that Jesus saw beyond the process was His seed: "Yet it pleased the LORD to bruise Him; He has put Him to grief. When You make His soul an offering for sin, He shall see His seed, ..." (Isa. 53:10, NJK). Jesus saw all of those who would be born again because of His death on the cross (cf. John 12:24, 32).

A third product that Jesus saw beyond the process was the satisfaction of the justice of God: "He shall see the labor of His soul, and be satisfied" (Isa. 53:11, NKJ). The justice of God says that the soul that sins shall die: "The soul who sins shall die" (Ezek. 18:4b, NKJ). "For the wages of sin is death, but the gift of God is eternal life in Christ Jesus our Lord" (Rom. 6:23, NKJ).

When Jesus died on the cross as our substitute, He satisfied the justice of God:

Surely He has borne our griefs and carried our sorrows; yet we esteemed Him stricken, smitten by God, and afflicted. But He was wounded for our transgressions, He was bruised for our iniquities; The chastisement for our peace was upon Him, and by His stripes we are healed. All we like sheep have gone astray; we have turned, every one, to his own way; and the Lord has laid on Him the iniquity of us all (Isa. 53:4-6, NKJ). Whom God set forth as a propitiation by His blood, through faith, to demonstrate His righteousness, because in His forbearance God had passed over the sins that were previously committed, to demonstrate at the present time His righteousness, that He might be just and the justifier of the one who has faith in Jesus (Rom. 3:25-26, NKJ).

And according to the law almost all things are purified with blood, and without shedding of blood there is no remission (Heb. 9:22, NKJ). And He Himself is the propitiation for our sins, and not for ours only but also for the whole world (1 John 2:2, NKJ).

A fourth product of the process that Jesus saw was Sunday: "He shall prolong His days, and the pleasure of the LORD shall prosper in His hand" (Isa. 53:10, NJK). When Jesus was beaten beyond recognition (Isa. 52:14; cf. Matt. 26:67), when a crown of thorns was placed upon His head, when He was scourged (John 19:1), Jesus knew that Resurrection Sunday was coming after the Crucifixion on Friday:

For as Jonah was three days and three nights in the belly of the great fish, so will the Son of Man be three days and three nights in the

heart of the earth (Matt. 12:40, NKJ). Now Jesus, going up to Jerusalem, took the twelve disciples aside on the road and said to them, "Behold, we are going up to Jerusalem, and the Son of Man will be betrayed to the chief priests and to the scribes; and they will condemn Him to death, and deliver Him to the Gentiles to mock and to scourge and to crucify. And the third day He will rise again" (Matt. 20:17-19, NKJ).

Jesus answered and said to them, "Destroy this temple, and in three days I will raise it up." Then the Jews said, "It has taken forty-six years to build this temple, and will You raise it up in three days?" But He was speaking of the temple of His body (John 2:19-21, NKJ).

Discussion Questions
Chapter 7

1. What were some of the things that Job did that helped him to go through the storms in his life?

2. What were some of the things Jesus saw beyond the cross that helped Him endure the cross?

Reflections

1. Can you recall some of the factors that assisted you in going through a storm in your life?

2. Can you recall some of the products that resulted from the process of going through a storm?

Notes

Chapter 8

How to Prepare for Storms

Since we all will encounter a storm on this voyage of life before our final destination is reached, it is important that we prepare as best as we can before the storms come.

One of the ways that we can prepare for storms is to develop a consistent devotional life. I believe that one of the factors that helped Job get through his storm without going insane was his devotional life prior to the storm:

And his sons would go and feast in their houses, each on his appointed day, and would send and invite their three sisters to eat and drink with them. So it was, when the days of feasting had run their course, that Job would send and sanctify them, and he would rise early in the morning and offer burnt offerings according to the number of them all. For Job said, "It may be that my sons have sinned and cursed God in their hearts." Thus Job did regularly (Job 1:4-5, NKJ).

I have not departed from the commandment of His lips; I have treasured the words of His mouth more than my necessary food (Job 23:12, NKJ).

Some of the other servants of God who had consistent

devotional lives that prepared them for their storms were David (Ps. 5:3; 55:17; 63:1-8), Daniel (Dan. 6:10), Nehemiah(Neh. 1:4-7, 11; 2:4; 4:9; 5:19; 6:9, 14), Paul and Silas (Acts 16:13, 25).

Jesus commanded His disciples to "watch and pray" in order to be prepared for the storms that they were about to face (Matt. 26:41).

Daily devotion should include prayer, worship, and the Word of God. Many Bible scholars recommend the acronym ACTS as a guide to how to pray: Adoration, Confession, Thanksgiving, and Supplication. Note Paul's command in Philippians 4:6, "Be anxious for nothing, but in everything by prayer and supplication, with thanksgiving, let your request be made known to God." According to Warren Wiersbe, the word "prayer" in this verse is a translation of a Greek word that "carries the idea of adoration, devotion, and worship." (Wiersbe, W. W. 1996, c1989. The Bible exposition commentary. "An exposition of the New Testament comprising the entire 'BE' series" Victor Books: Wheaton, Ill.)

Next is Confession (Prov. 28:13; cf. Ps. 23:1-5; 1 John 1:9). Then there is Thanksgiving (1 Thess. 5:18; cf. Ps. 100:4; 136:1-26). Finally, there is Supplication, which involves petitions in relation to the problem or provisions.

The Word of God is a necessary part of one's daily

devotion. God said to Joshua, "This Book of the Law shall not depart from your mouth, but you shall meditate in it day and night, that you may observe to do according to all that is written in it. For then you will make your way prosperous, and then you will have good success" (Joshua 1:8, NKJ). Jesus said: "It is written, 'Man shall not live by bread alone, but by every word that proceeds from the mouth of God' " (Matt. 4:4, NKJ).

Job said: "I have not departed from the commandment of His lips; I have treasured the words of His mouth more than my necessary food" (Job 23:12, NKJ). In the Septuagint Version, which is the Greek translation of the Old Testament, "words" is a translation of "rhema," which is a specific word. "Rhema" is also translated "word" in Romans 10:17, "So then faith comes by hearing, and hearing by the word [rhema] of God." Job valued the Word of God more than food for his physical body.

Paul wrote in 2 Timothy 3:16-17, NKJ: "All Scripture is given by inspiration of God, and is profitable for doctrine, for reproof, for correction, for instruction in righteousness, that the man of God may be complete, thoroughly equipped for every good work."

A second factor that helps to prepare us for storms is obedience to the Word of God. Strength comes from obedience:

Therefore you shall keep every commandment which I command you today, that you may be strong, and go in and possess the land which you cross over to possess (Deut. 11:8, NKJ).

Jesus said, **"Therefore whoever hears these sayings of Mine, and does them, I will liken him to a wise man who built his house on the rock: and the rain descended, the floods came, and the winds blew and beat on that house; and it did not fall, for it was founded on the rock. But everyone who hears these sayings of Mine, and does not do them, will be like a foolish man who built his house on the sand: and the rain descended, the floods came, and the winds blew and beat on that house; and it fell. And great was its fall"** (Matt. 7:24-27, NKJ).

Job was strong because of his obedience to the word of God: "My foot has held fast to His steps; I have kept His way and not turned aside. I have not departed from the command- ment of His lips; I have treasured the words of His mouth more than my necessary food" (Job 23:11-12, NKJ).

A third factor that helps to prepare us for storms is rest. Elijah was not prepared for one of the storms in his life because of a lack of rest. Elijah became depressed and discour- aged because he was exhausted physically, emotionally, and spiritually. No doubt the contest with the prophets of Baal on Mount Carmel was spiritually exhausting (1 Kings 18:19-40). Then Elijah outran Ahab's chariot for over 15 miles from Mount Carmel to Jezreel. This no doubt was physically exhausting (1 Kings 18:41-46).

Notice that God first gave Elijah what he needed most: rest, food, and water:

Then as he lay and slept under a broom tree, suddenly an angel touched him, and said to him, "Arise and eat." Then he looked, and there by his head was a cake baked on coals, and a jar of water. So he ate and drank, and lay down again. And the angel of the LORD came back the second time, and touched him, and said, "Arise and eat, because the journey is too great for you." So he arose, and ate and drank; and he went in the strength of that food forty days and forty nights as far as Horeb, the mountain of God (1 Kings 19:5-8, NKJ).

Rest and relaxation help to prepare us for storms. Rest helps the immune system to function properly. When the immune system breaks down because of a lack of rest, we become more susceptible to illness.

When we are exhausted, we tend to become more impatient and more easily irritated. Moreover, our attitude and outlook on life change when we are exhausted. Jesus encouraged His disciples to rest:

Then the apostles gathered to Jesus and told Him all things, both what they had done and what they had taught. And He said to them, "Come aside by yourselves to a deserted place and rest a while." For there were many coming and going, and they did not even have time

to eat. **So they departed to a deserted place in the boat by themselves (Mark 6:30-32, NKJ).**

We should practice the Sabbath Principle: Work six days and rest one day (Gen. 2:1-3; Ex. 20:8-11). Our bodies are temples of the Holy Spirit, and God wants us to be good stewards of the temple of the Holy Spirit:

Or do you not know that your body is the temple of the Holy Spirit who is in you, whom you have from God, and you are not your own? For you were bought at a price; therefore glorify God in your body and in your spirit, which are God's (1 Cor. 6:19-20, NKJ).

A fourth factor that will help to prepare us for storms is fellowship with other believers. The word "fellowship" is a translation to the Greek word "Koinonia," which means "having in common" and "to share." We have a common Savior - Jesus Christ. Fellowship involves the sharing of our beliefs, blessings, and burdens. Fellowship with other believers is one of the requirements for spiritual growth. One of the benefits of fellowship is the mutual encouragement of one another:

Let us hold fast the confession of our hope without wavering, for He who promised is faithful. And let us consider one another in order to stir up love and good works, not forsaking the assembling of ourselves together, as is the manner of some, but exhorting one another, and so much the more as you see the Day approaching (Heb. 10:23-

25, NKJ).

Fellowship was one of the factors that prepared the early church for the storms that were encountered:

And they continued steadfastly in the apostles' doctrine and fellowship, in the breaking of bread, and in prayers (Acts 2:42, NKJ).

And being let go, they went to their own companions and reported all that the chief priests and elders had said to them. So when they heard that, they raised their voice to God with one accord and said: "Lord, You are God, who made heaven and earth and the sea, and all that is in them, who by the mouth of Your servant David have said: 'Why did the nations rage, and the people plot vain things? The kings of the earth took their stand, and the rulers were gathered together against the Lord and against His Christ.' For truly against Your holy Servant Jesus, whom You anointed, both Herod and Pontius Pilate, with the Gentiles and the people of Israel, were gathered together to do whatever Your hand and Your purpose determined before to be done. Now, Lord, look on their threats, and grant to Your servants that with all boldness they may speak Your word, by stretching out Your hand to heal, and that signs and wonders may be done through the name of Your holy Servant Jesus." And when they had prayed, the place where they were assembled together was shaken; and they were all filled with the Holy Spirit, and they spoke the word of God with boldness (Acts 4:23-31, NKJ).

When we are facing a storm, it is good to have someone

to whom we can turn for prayer and encouragement.

Elijah isolated himself from the fellowship of other believers. After receiving a threatening message from Jezebel, Elijah left his servant at Beersheba and went alone into the wilderness:

Then Jezebel sent a messenger to Elijah, saying, "So let the gods do to me, and more also, if I do not make your life as the life of one of them by tomorrow about this time." And when he saw that, he arose and ran for his life, and went to Beersheba, which belongs to Judah, and left his servant there. But he himself went a day's journey into the wilderness, and came and sat down under a broom tree. And he prayed that he might die, and said, "It is enough! Now, LORD, take my life, for I am no better than my fathers!" (1 Kings 19:2-4, NKJ).

Elijah believed that he was the only believer faithful to God:

And there he went into a cave, and spent the night in that place; and behold, the word of the LORD came to him, and He said to him, "What are you doing here, Elijah?" So he said, "I have been very zealous for the LORD God of hosts; for the children of Israel have forsaken Your covenant, torn down Your altars, and killed Your prophets with the sword. I alone am left; and they seek to take my life" (1 Kings 19:9-10, NKJ).

God informed Elijah that he was not the only faithful servant in Israel: "Yet I have reserved seven thousand in Israel, all whose knees have not bowed to Baal, and every mouth that has not kissed him" (1 Kings 19:18, NKJ).

Discussion Questions
Chapter 8

1. What are some steps that you believe you can take that will help to prepare you for a storm in your life?

2. What are some of the steps that Elijah could have taken that might have prepared him for the storm in his life?

3. What prepared David, Daniel, Job and other servants of God for the storms in their lives?

Reflections

1. Can you recall some of the things that prepared you to go through a storm in your life?

2. Can you recall one thing that was the most helpful to you in the midst of your storm?

Notes

Chapter 9

How to Comfort Victims of Storms

We have seen that no one is exempt from storms no matter how good or godly he or she may be. We have seen that storms do not always mean that one is being punished for one's own personal sins. We have seen that Satan can cause storms with God's permission. Remember that God is sovereign over storms. We have seen that storms disclose many things about the victim and about others.

In this chapter, we will examine some ways of comforting victims of storms. What do you say to a person like Job? God said that Job was more righteous than anyone else in the land. Job was a man who avoided evil. Job was a priest in his home; he prayed regularly for his family. Job esteemed the words of God more than his necessary food. From the panorama of Job's life recorded in Job 29:1 - 31:40, we learn that Job trained his eyes not to look lustful at a young woman. Job loved God more than life itself; he was eyes for the blind and feet for the lame; he cared for the poor and needy; and he defended widows and the fatherless. Although God said that there was none in the land more righteous than Job, in one day Job lost seven sons and three daughters along with all of his material possessions. Then Job later lost his health. Again, what do you say to a person like Job?

When Job's three friends appeared to comfort him, they were silent for seven days and seven nights. They did not say anything to Job. They were just present. The three friends of Job were good comforters until they began to speak. They ceased to be good comforters when they sought to answer the question, "Why?" There are times when there is no satisfactory answer to "Why?" From the three friends of Job, we learn some things to do and some things not to do to comfort victims of storms. How does one comfort the victim of a storm?

BE PRESENT WITH THE VICTIM OF A STORM

Job's three friends demonstrated care, concern, and compassion by their physical presence with him: "Now when Job's three friends heard of all this adversity that had come upon him, each one came from his own place Eliphaz the Temanite, Bildad the Shuhite, and Zophar the Naamathite. For they had made an appointment together to come and mourn with him, and to comfort him. And when they raised their eyes from afar, and did not recognize him, they lifted their voices and wept;

and each one tore his robe and sprinkled dust on his head toward heaven" (Job 2:11-12, NKJ).

Paul tells us in 1 Corinthians 1:3-4 that God is the God of all comfort. God has many ways of comforting us. One way that God comforts is by His presence. David said, "Yea, though I walk through the valley of the shadow of death, I will fear no evil; For You are with me; Your rod and Your staff, they comfort me" (Ps. 23:4, NKJ).

A second way that God comforts is by His promises:

But now, thus says the Lord, who created you, O Jacob, and He who formed you, O Israel: "Fear not, for I have redeemed you; I have called you by your name; you are mine. When you pass through the waters, I will be with you; and through the rivers, they shall not overflow you. When you walk through the fire, you shall not be burned, nor shall the flame scorch you" (Isa. 43:1-2, NKJ).

This is my comfort in my affliction, for Your word has given me life (Ps. 119:50, NKJ).

A third way that God comforts is by the physical presence of others. God comforted Paul with the physical presence of Titus: "Nevertheless God, who comforts the downcast, comforted us by the coming of Titus" (2 Cor. 7:6, NKJ).

In Job 2:12, Job's three friends demonstrated the signs or symbols of mourning: They tore their clothes, and they sprinkled dust upon their heads toward heaven. Paul tells us in Romans 12:15, "Rejoice with those who rejoice, and weep with those who weep."

According to Ecclesiastes 3:7, there is a time to speak and a time to be silent. When comforting the victim of a storm, let speech be the exception and let silence be the rule. Job's three friends were good comforters until they began to speak. Observe Job's rebuke of his three friends because of some of the things they had to say:

But you forgers of lies, you are all worthless physicians. Oh, that you would be silent, and it would be your wisdom! (Job 13:4-5, NKJ).

Then Job answered and said: "I have heard many such things; miserable comforters are you all! Shall words of wind have an end? Or what provokes you that you answer? I also could speak as you do, if your soul were in my soul's place. I could heap up words against you, and shake my head at you; but I would strengthen you with my mouth, and the comfort of my lips would relieve your grief" (Job 16:1-5, NKJ).

God also rebuked Job's friends for what they said:

And so it was, after the Lord had spoken these words to Job, that the LORD said to Eliphaz the Temanite, "My wrath is aroused against you and your two friends, for you have not spoken of Me what is right, as My servant Job has" (Job 42:7, NKJ).

When seeking to comfort a victim of a storm, just be present. If God gives you something to say, then say it. Otherwise be silent. The right words can be helpful. On the other hand, the wrong words can be harmful: "Death and life are in the power of the tongue, and those who love it will eat its fruit" (Prov. 18:21, NKJ). "A word fitly spoken is like apples of gold in settings of silver" (Prov. 25:11, NKJ).

Saying that a deceased person is in a better place is not always comforting to everyone. After preaching a sermon on "How to Comfort Victims of Trials," a couple whose son had been deceased for about a year came to me at the end of the service and thanked me for the message. They informed me that it was painful for people to tell them that their child was in a better place because those words made them feel that they had not done their very best for their child.

BE PATIENT WITH THE VICTIM OF A STORM

Job's three friends were patient for seven days and seven nights: "So they sat down with him on the ground seven days and seven nights, and no one spoke a word to him, for they saw that his grief was very great" (Job 2:13, NKJ).

Job did not curse God, but he did curse the day of his birth in chapter 3. Victims of storms may say and do strange things.

Be patient with them. Patiently listen to what is said and what is not being said. When people are going through a storm, they may say and do things that are not characteristic of them. There may also be drastic changes in their appearance. Job's friends did not recognize Job because of the change in his appearance:

And when they raised their eyes from afar, and did not recognize him, they lifted their voices and wept; and each one tore his robe and sprinkled dust on his head toward heaven (Job 2:12, NKJ).

BE PRACTICAL WITH THE VICTIM OF A STORM

Be sensitive to the needs of the victim of a storm. At the end of seven days and seven nights, Job's three friends were insensitive to his needs. Job needed words of comfort not words of criticism. Job's friends insisted that his storm was due to some sin he had committed and had not confessed.

Be practical. The greatest and immediate needs of the victim of a storm may be the basic necessities of life, such as food, water, clothing, and rest. When Elijah fled from Jezebel and became so depressed that he wanted to die, God provided him with food, water, and rest before He gave him his next assignment (1 Kings 19:4-18).

Paul comforted 275 passengers on a ship in a storm by

encouraging them to eat some food after they had been without food for fourteen days:

And as day was about to dawn, Paul implored them all to take food, saying, "Today is the fourteenth day you have waited and continued without food, and eaten nothing. Therefore I urge you to take nourishment, for this is for your survival, since not a hair will fall from the head of any of you." And when he had said these things, he took bread and gave thanks to God in the presence of them all; and when he had broken it he began to eat. Then they were all encouraged, and also took food themselves. And in all we were two hundred and seventy-six persons on the ship (Acts 27:33-37, NKJ).

Both James and John tell us to show our faith and love by meeting the basic needs of others:

If a brother or sister is naked and destitute of daily food, and one of you says to them, "Depart in peace, be warmed and filled," but you do not give them the things which are needed for the body, what does it profit? Thus also faith by itself, if it does not have works, is dead (James 2:15-17, NKJ). But whoever has this world's goods, and sees his brother in need, and shuts up his heart from him, how does the love of God abide in him? My little children, let us not love in word or in tongue, but in deed and in truth (1 John 3:17-18, NKJ).

BE PRAYERFUL WITH THE VICTIM OF A STORM

Pray for and with the victim of a storm. There is nothing to indicate that Job's three friends were prayerful. Pray that God will give grace to the victim of a storm and that God will give grace and wisdom to you so that you can comfort the victim of a storm. Pray that God will give you the right words. Pray that God will give you wisdom as to when to speak and when to be silent. Remember also that the wrong words can do more harm than good (Job 13:4-5; 16:2). On the other hand, the right words spoken at the right time can be comforting: "But I would strengthen you with my mouth, and the comfort of my lips would relieve your grief" (Job 16:5, NKJ).

In the year 2006, I encountered more storms than in any previous year. I will mention three: In May of 2006, my mother went home to be with the Lord. About a year before she died, she requested that I preach her funeral if possible and if I outlived her. In July of 2006, I underwent surgery for prostate cancer. In December of 2006, my wife of over 50 years had emergency surgery for a brain aneurysm. Prior to the surgery, she suffered for over a week with a severe headache. Three different doctors treated her for a migraine headache and sent her home. Finally, a fourth doctor performed the necessary tests to determine the cause of her headache.

During the storms in my life, I found comfort in the presence and prayers of God's people. I did not find comfort in being reminded of my past sermons because, to me, the reminders implied that I was not practicing what I had preached.

Discussion Questions
Chapter 9

1. What made Job's three friends good comforters for seven days and seven nights?

2. When did Job's three friends cease to be good comforters?

3. What were the factors that assisted Job in living without an answer to the question "why"?

Reflections

1. What did others say or do that comforted you in your storm?

2. Can you recall a storm for which there is no satisfactory answer to the question "why"?

Notes

About The Author

Julius R. Malone has been the Senior Pastor of the New Testament Church of Milwaukee since November, 1980. Malone and his wife Ann moved from Memphis, Tennessee to Milwaukee, Wisconsin in February, 1960. Malone served for several years as youth pastor of the New Hope Baptist Church under the late Pastor R. L. Lathan, and he later served as Assistant Pastor for over two years to the late Pastor Kenneth Bowen at the Mount Moriah Baptist Church. Malone attended the Chicago Baptist Institute of Theology for two years, and he taught for two years at the Milwaukee Institute of Theology. Malone holds a Bachelor of Science Degree and a Master of Science Degree in Social Work from the University of Wisconsin-Milwaukee. Prior to becoming a senior pastor, Malone worked for over six years as a Child Protective Service Social Worker for Milwaukee County. Pastor Malone has been a featured speaker for Christian Business Men's Annual Retreat at Green Lake, Wisconsin and Interlaken Resort at Lake Geneva, Wisconsin and Cedine Bible Camp in Spring City, Tennessee. He has also been a workshop presenter for The No Regrets Statewide Conference of Christian Men at Elmbrook Church in Brookfield, Wisconsin, and The Lakeland Baptist Association's annual Kingdom Growth Conference. Pastor Malone is featured daily on several radio stations in Wisconsin.

For speaking engagements, book signings, etc:
The New Testament Church Of Milwaukee
Pastor Julius R Malone
10201 W Bradley Rd. Milwaukee WI 53224
Office: (414)365-1690